# The Poetry of Thomas Gray

Thomas Gray was born on 26 December 1716 in Cornhill in London. His father was a scrivener and his mother a milliner. He was the fifth of twelve children and the only one to survive.

With his father becoming mentally unwell and abusing his wife she left with Thomas in tow for a safer life.

Thomas was sent to Eton, where two of his uncles worked, and although he was a delicate and scholarly child with an aversion to sports he found it suited him. Whilst there he made three close friends; Horace Walpole, son of the Prime Minister Robert Walpole; Thomas Ashton, and Richard West. The four prided themselves on their style, humour, and appreciation of beauty. They were called the "quadruple alliance."

In 1734 Gray went up to Peterhouse, Cambridge. Although his family wished him to study law he spent most of his time reading classical and modern literature, and playing Vivaldi and Scarlatti on the harpsichord for relaxation.

In 1738 he accompanied his old school-friend Walpole on his Grand Tour of Europe. It was Walpole who later helped publish Gray's poetry.

Gray began to seriously write poems in 1742, mainly after his close friend Richard West died. He moved to Cambridge and began a programme of literary study. Gray was a brilliant bookworm, a quiet, abstracted, dreaming scholar. He became a Fellow first of Peterhouse, and later of Pembroke College where he had moved after the students at Peterhouse played a prank on him.

It is thought that Gray began writing his masterpiece, the Elegy Written in a Country Churchyard, in the graveyard of St Giles parish church in Stoke Poges, Buckinghamshire, in 1742. After several years of leaving it unfinished, he completed it in 1750. When Gray sent it to Walpole, Walpole sent off the poem as a manuscript and it appeared in many magazines. Gray then published the poem himself and received the credit he was due. The poem was a literary sensation. Its reflective, calm and stoic tone was greatly admired, and despite the piracy it was imitated, quoted and translated into Latin and Greek.

Gray spent most of his life as a scholar in Cambridge, and only travelled again later in life. Although he wrote little he is regarded by some as the foremost English-language poet of the mid-18th century. In 1757, he was offered the post of Poet Laureate, which he refused.

Gray was extremely self-critical and feared failure. He once wrote that he feared his collected works would be "mistaken for the works of a flea". Gray came to be known as one of the "Graveyard poets" of the late 18th century, along with Oliver Goldsmith, William Cowper, and Christopher Smart. Gray perhaps knew these men, sharing ideas about death, mortality, and the finality of death.

In 1768, after the death of Lawrence Brockett the Regius chair of Modern History at Cambridge, a sinecure which carried a salary of £400, fell vacant and Gray secured the position.

Thomas Gray died on 30 July 1771 in Cambridge, and was buried beside his mother in the churchyard of Stoke Poges, the setting for his famous Elegy.

## Index Of Poems
ON THE SPRING
ON THE DEATH OF A FAVOURITE CAT, DROWNED IN A TUB OF GOLDD FISHES
ON A DISTANT PROSPECT OF ETON COLLEGE
THE PROGRESS OF POESY
THE BARD
HYMN TO ADVERSITY.
TOPHET
SKETCH OF HIS OWN CHARACTER
LINES WRITTEN AT BURNHAM
LINES SPOKEN BY THE GHOST OF JOHN DENNIS AT THE DEVIL TAVERN
EPITAPH ON SIR WILLIAM WILLIAMS
EPITAPH ON MRS MASON
EPITAPH ON MRS CLERKE
EPITAPH ON A CHILD
THE CANDIDATE
LINES ON THE ACCESSION OF GEORGE III
SATIRE ON THE HEADS OF HOUSES; OR, NEVER A BARREL THE BETTER HERRING
THE PROGRESS OF POESY
THE FATAL SISTERS
THE CURSE UPON EDWARD
SONNET ON THE DEATH OF MR RICHARD WEST
ODE ON THE PLEASURE ARISING FROM VICISSITUDE
ODE ON A DISTANT PROSPECT OF ETON COLLEGE
THE LIFE OF THOMAS GRAY BY ROBERT CARRUTHERS.
STOKE-POGIS - FROM HOWITT'S "HOMES AND HAUNTS OF THE BRITISH POETS."

ELEGY WRITTEN IN A COUNTRY CHURCHYARD.
The curfew tolls the knell of parting day,
The lowing herd wind slowly o'er the lea,
The plowman homeward plods his weary way,
And leaves the world to darkness and to me.

Now fades the glimmering landscape on the sight,
And all the air a solemn stillness holds,
Save where the beetle wheels his droning flight,
And drowsy tinklings lull the distant folds:

Save that, from yonder ivy-mantled tower,
The moping owl does to the moon complain
Of such as, wandering near her secret bower,
Molest her ancient solitary reign.

Beneath those rugged elms, that yew-tree's shade,
Where heaves the turf in many a mouldering heap,
Each in his narrow cell forever laid,
The rude forefathers of the hamlet sleep.

The breezy call of incense-breathing morn,
The swallow twittering from the straw-built shed,
The cock's shrill clarion, or the echoing horn,
No more shall rouse them from their lowly bed.

For them no more the blazing hearth shall burn,
Or busy housewife ply her evening care;
No children run to lisp their sire's return,
Or climb his knees the envied kiss to share.

Oft did the harvest to their sickle yield,
Their furrow oft the stubborn glebe has broke;
How jocund did they drive their team afield!
How bow'd the woods beneath their sturdy stroke!

Let not Ambition mock their useful toil,
Their homely joys, and destiny obscure;
Nor Grandeur hear with a disdainful smile
The short and simple annals of the poor.

The boast of heraldry, the pomp of power,
And all that beauty, all that wealth e'er gave,
Awaits alike th' inevitable hour.
The paths of glory lead but to the grave.

Nor you, ye proud, impute to these the fault,
If Memory o'er their tomb no trophies raise;
Where, through the long-drawn aisle and fretted vault,
The pealing anthem swells the note of praise.

Can storied urn or animated bust
Back to its mansion call the fleeting breath?
Can Honour's voice provoke the silent dust?
Or Flattery soothe the dull cold ear of Death?

Perhaps in this neglected spot is laid
Some heart once pregnant with celestial fire;
Hands, that the rod of empire might have sway'd,
Or wak'd to ecstasy the living lyre:

But Knowledge to their eyes her ample page,
Rich with the spoils of time, did ne'er unroll;
Chill Penury repress'd their noble rage,
And froze the genial current of the soul.

Full many a gem of purest ray serene
The dark unfathom'd caves of ocean bear;
Full many a flower is born to blush unseen,
And waste its sweetness on the desert air.

Some village Hampden, that with dauntless breast

The little tyrant of his fields withstood,
Some mute inglorious Milton here may rest,
Some Cromwell, guiltless of his country's blood.

Th' applause of listening senates to command,
The threats of pain and ruin to despise,
To scatter plenty o'er a smiling land,
And read their history in a nation's eyes,

Their lot forbade: nor circumscrib'd alone
Their growing virtues, but their crimes confin'd;
Forbade to wade through slaughter to a throne,
And shut the gates of mercy on mankind,

The struggling pangs of conscious truth to hide,
To quench the blushes of ingenuous shame,
Or heap the shrine of Luxury and Pride
With incense kindled at the Muse's flame.

Far from the madding crowd's ignoble strife,
Their sober wishes never learn'd to stray;
Along the cool sequester'd vale of life
They kept the noiseless tenor of their way.

Yet even these bones from insult to protect,
Some frail memorial still erected nigh,
With uncouth rhymes and shapeless sculpture deck'd,
Implores the passing tribute of a sigh.

Their name, their years, spelt by th' unletter'd Muse,
The place of fame and elegy supply;
And many a holy text around she strews,
That teach the rustic moralist to die.

For who, to dumb forgetfulness a prey,
This pleasing anxious being e'er resign'd,
Left the warm precincts of the cheerful day,
Nor cast one longing lingering look behind?

On some fond breast the parting soul relies,
Some pious drops the closing eye requires;
Even from the tomb the voice of Nature cries,
Even in our ashes live their wonted fires.

For thee, who, mindful of th' unhonour'd dead,
Dost in these lines their artless tale relate,
If chance, by lonely contemplation led,
Some kindred spirit shall inquire thy fate,

Haply some hoary-headed swain may say,
"Oft have we seen him at the peep of dawn

Brushing with hasty steps the dews away,
To meet the sun upon the upland lawn.

"There at the foot of yonder nodding beech,
That wreathes its old fantastic roots so high,
His listless length at noontide would he stretch,
And pore upon the brook that babbles by.

"Hard by yon wood, now smiling as in scorn,
Muttering his wayward fancies he would rove;
Now drooping, woeful-wan, like one forlorn,
Or craz'd with care, or cross'd in hopeless love.

"One morn I miss'd him on the custom'd hill,
Along the heath, and near his favourite tree;
Another came; nor yet beside the rill,
Nor up the lawn, nor at the wood was he;

"The next, with dirges due in sad array,
Slow through the church-way path we saw him borne.
Approach and read (for thou canst read) the lay
Grav'd on the stone beneath yon aged thorn."

**THE EPITAPH**
Here rests his head upon the lap of Earth
A youth, to Fortune and to Fame unknown;
Fair Science frown'd not on his humble birth,
And Melancholy mark'd him for her own.

Large was his bounty, and his soul sincere,
Heaven did a recompense as largely send;
He gave to Misery all he had, a tear;
He gain'd from Heaven ('twas all he wish'd) a friend.

No farther seek his merits to disclose,
Or draw his frailties from their dread abode,
(There they alike in trembling hope repose)
The bosom of his Father and his God.


ON THE SPRING
Lo! where the rosy-bosom'd Hours,
Fair Venus' train, appear,
Disclose the long-expecting flowers,
And wake the purple year!
The Attic warbler pours her throat,
Responsive to the cuckoo's note,
The untaught harmony of spring;
While, whispering pleasure as they fly,
Cool Zephyrs thro' the clear blue sky

Their gather'd fragrance fling.

Where'er the oak's thick branches stretch
A broader browner shade,
Where'er the rude and moss-grown beech
O'ercanopies the glade,
Beside some water's rushy brink
With me the Muse shall sit, and think
(At ease reclin'd in rustic state)
How vain the ardour of the crowd,
How low, how little are the proud,
How indigent the great!

Still is the toiling hand of Care;
The panting herds repose:
Yet hark, how thro' the peopled air
The busy murmur glows!
The insect youth are on the wing,
Eager to taste the honied spring,
And float amid the liquid noon:
Some lightly o'er the current skim,
Some show their gayly-gilded trim
Quick-glancing to the sun.

To Contemplation's sober eye
Such is the race of Man;
And they that creep, and they that fly,
Shall end where they began.
Alike the busy and the gay
But flutter thro' life's little day,
In Fortune's varying colours drest:
Brush'd by the hand of rough Mischance,
Or chill'd by age, their airy dance
They leave, in dust to rest.

Methinks I hear in accents low
The sportive kind reply:
Poor moralist! and what art thou?
A solitary fly!
Thy joys no glittering female meets,
No hive hast thou of hoarded sweets,
No painted plumage to display:
On hasty wings thy youth is flown;
Thy sun is set, thy spring is gone--
We frolic while 'tis May.

**ON THE DEATH OF A FAVOURITE CAT, DROWNED IN A TUB OF GOLDD FISHES**
'Twas on a lofty vase's side,
Where China's gayest art had dyed

The azure flowers that blow;
Demurest of the tabby kind,
The pensive Selima, reclin'd,
Gaz'd on the lake below.

Her conscious tail her joy declar'd:
The fair round face, the snowy beard,
The velvet of her paws,
Her coat, that with the tortoise vies,
Her ears of jet, and emerald eyes,
She saw; and purr'd applause.

Still had she gaz'd; but midst the tide
Two angel forms were seen to glide,
The Genii of the stream:
Their scaly armour's Tyrian hue
Through richest purple to the view
Betray'd a golden gleam.

The hapless nymph with wonder saw:
A whisker first, and then a claw,
With many an ardent wish,
She stretch'd in vain to reach the prize.
What female heart can gold despise?
What Cat's averse to fish?

Presumptuous maid! with looks intent
Again she stretch'd, again she bent,
Nor knew the gulf between.
(Malignant Fate sat by, and smil'd.)
The slippery verge her feet beguil'd,
She tumbled headlong in.

Eight times emerging from the flood,
She mew'd to every watery God,
Some speedy aid to send.
No Dolphin came, no Nereid stirr'd:
Nor cruel Tom, nor Susan heard.
A favourite has no friend!

From hence, ye beauties, undeceiv'd,
Know, one false step is ne'er retriev'd,
And be with caution bold.
Not all that tempts your wandering eyes
And heedless hearts is lawful prize,
Nor all that glisters gold.


ON A DISTANT PROSPECT OF ETON COLLEGE
Ye distant spires, ye antique towers,

That crown the watery glade,
Where grateful Science still adores
Her Henry's holy shade;
And ye, that from the stately brow
Of Windsor's heights th' expanse below
Of grove, of lawn, of mead survey,
Whose turf, whose shade, whose flowers among
Wanders the hoary Thames along
His silver-winding way:

Ah, happy hills! ah, pleasing shade!
Ah, fields belov'd in vain!
Where once my careless childhood stray'd,
A stranger yet to pain!
I feel the gales that from ye blow
A momentary bliss bestow,
As, waving fresh their gladsome wing,
My weary soul they seem to soothe,
And, redolent of joy and youth,
To breathe a second spring.

Say, Father Thames, for thou hast seen
Full many a sprightly race
Disporting on thy margent green
The paths of pleasure trace;
Who foremost now delight to cleave
With pliant arm thy glassy wave?
The captive linnet which enthrall?
What idle progeny succeed
To chase the rolling circle's speed,
Or urge the flying ball?

While some, on earnest business bent,
Their murmuring labours ply
'Gainst graver hours that bring constraint
To sweeten liberty,
Some bold adventurers disdain
The limits of their little reign,
And unknown regions dare descry:
Still as they run they look behind,
They hear a voice in every wind,
And snatch a fearful joy.

Gay hope is theirs by fancy fed,
Less pleasing when possest;
The tear forgot as soon as shed,
The sunshine of the breast:
Theirs buxom health of rosy hue,
Wild wit, invention ever new,
And lively cheer of vigour born;
The thoughtless day, the easy night,

The spirits pure, the slumbers light,
That fly th' approach of morn.

Alas! regardless of their doom,
The little victims play;
No sense have they of ills to come,
No care beyond to-day:
Yet see how all around 'em wait
The ministers of human fate,
And black Misfortune's baleful train!
Ah, show them where in ambush stand
To seize their prey the murtherous band!
Ah, tell them, they are men!

These shall the fury Passions tear,
The vultures of the mind,
Disdainful Anger, pallid Fear,
And Shame that skulks behind;
Or pining Love shall waste their youth,
Or Jealousy with rankling tooth,
That inly gnaws the secret heart;
And Envy wan, and faded Care,
Grim-visag'd comfortless Despair,
And Sorrow's piercing dart.

Ambition this shall tempt to rise,
Then whirl the wretch from high,
To bitter Scorn a sacrifice,
And grinning Infamy.
The stings of Falsehood those shall try,
And hard Unkindness' alter'd eye,
That mocks the tear it forc'd to flow;
And keen Remorse with blood defil'd,
And moody Madness laughing wild
Amid severest woe.

Lo! in the vale of years beneath
A grisly troop are seen,
The painful family of Death,
More hideous than their queen:
This racks the joints, this fires the veins,
That every labouring sinew strains,
Those in the deeper vitals rage:
Lo! Poverty, to fill the band,
That numbs the soul with icy hand,
And slow-consuming Age.

To each his sufferings: all are men,
Condemn'd alike to groan;
The tender for another's pain,
Th' unfeeling for his own.

Yet, ah! why should they know their fate,
Since sorrow never comes too late,
And happiness too swiftly flies?
Thought would destroy their paradise.
No more;--where ignorance is bliss,
'Tis folly to be wise.


THE PROGRESS OF POESY.
A Pindaric Ode

I. I
Awake, Æolian lyre, awake,
And give to rapture all thy trembling strings.
From Helicon's harmonious springs
A thousand rills their mazy progress take:
The laughing flowers that round them blow,
Drink life and fragrance as they flow.
Now the rich stream of music winds along,
Deep, majestic, smooth, and strong,
Thro' verdant vales, and Ceres' golden reign:
Now rolling down the steep amain,
Headlong, impetuous, see it pour;
The rocks and nodding groves rebellow to the roar.

I. II
Oh! Sovereign of the willing soul,
Parent of sweet and solemn-breathing airs,
Enchanting shell! the sullen Cares
And frantic Passions hear thy soft control.
On Thracia's hills the Lord of War
Has curb'd the fury of his car,
And dropt his thirsty lance at thy command.
Perching on the sceptred hand
Of Jove, thy magic lulls the feather'd king
With ruffled plumes and flagging wing:
Quench'd in dark clouds of slumber lie
The terror of his beak, and lightnings of his eye.

I. III
Thee the voice, the dance, obey,
Temper'd to thy warbled lay.
O'er Idalia's velvet-green
The rosy-crowned Loves are seen
On Cytherea's day
With antic Sports, and blue-eyed Pleasures,
Frisking light in frolic measures;
Now pursuing, now retreating,
Now in circling troops they meet:
To brisk notes in cadence beating,

Glance their many-twinkling feet.
Slow melting strains their Queen's approach declare:
Where'er she turns the Graces homage pay.
With arms sublime, that float upon the air,
In gliding state she wins her easy way:
O'er her warm cheek, and rising bosom, move
The bloom of young Desire and purple light of Love.

II. I
Man's feeble race what ills await!
Labour, and Penury, the racks of Pain,
Disease, and Sorrow's weeping train,
And Death, sad refuge from the storms of Fate!
The fond complaint, my song, disprove,
And justify the laws of Jove.
Say, has he given in vain the heavenly Muse?
Night and all her sickly dews,
Her spectres wan, and birds of boding cry,
He gives to range the dreary sky;
Till down the eastern cliffs afar
Hyperion's march they spy, and glittering shafts of war.

II. II
In climes beyond the solar road,
Where shaggy forms o'er ice-built mountains roam,
The Muse has broke the twilight gloom
To cheer the shivering native's dull abode.
And oft, beneath the odorous shade
Of Chili's boundless forests laid,
She deigns to hear the savage youth repeat,
In loose numbers wildly sweet,
Their feather-cinctur'd chiefs, and dusky loves.
Her track, where'er the Goddess roves,
Glory pursue, and generous Shame,
Th' unconquerable Mind, and Freedom's holy flame.

II. III
Woods, that wave o'er Delphi's steep,
Isles, that crown th' Ægean deep,
Fields, that cool Ilissus laves,
Or where Mæander's amber waves
In lingering labyrinths creep,
How do your tuneful echoes languish,
Mute, but to the voice of anguish!
Where each old poetic mountain
Inspiration breath'd around;
Every shade and hallow'd fountain
Murmur'd deep a solemn sound:
Till the sad Nine, in Greece's evil hour,
Left their Parnassus for the Latian plains.
Alike they scorn the pomp of tyrant Power,

And coward Vice, that revels in her chains.
When Latium had her lofty spirit lost,
They sought, O Albion! next thy sea-encircled coast.

III. I
Far from the sun and summer gale,
In thy green lap was Nature's darling laid,
What time, where lucid Avon stray'd,
To him the mighty mother did unveil
Her awful face: the dauntless child
Stretch'd forth his little arms and smil'd.
"This pencil take (she said), whose colours clear
Richly paint the vernal year:
Thine too these golden keys, immortal Boy!
This can unlock the gates of joy;
Of horror that, and thrilling fears,
Or ope the sacred source of sympathetic tears."

III. II
Nor second He, that rode sublime
Upon the seraph wings of Ecstasy,
The secrets of th' abyss to spy.
He pass'd the flaming bounds of place and time:
The living throne, the sapphire blaze,
Where angels tremble while they gaze,
He saw; but, blasted with excess of light,
Clos'd his eyes in endless night.
Behold, where Dryden's less presumptuous car,
Wide o'er the fields of glory bear
Two coursers of ethereal race,
With necks in thunder cloth'd, and long-resounding pace.

III. III
Hark, his hands the lyre explore!
Bright-eyed Fancy hovering o'er
Scatters from her pictur'd urn
Thoughts that breathe, and words that burn.
But ah! 'tis heard no more
Oh! lyre divine, what daring spirit
Wakes thee now? Tho' he inherit
Nor the pride, nor ample pinion,
That the Theban eagle bear,
Sailing with supreme dominion
Thro' the azure deep of air,
Yet oft before his infant eyes would run
Such forms as glitter in the Muse's ray
With orient hues, unborrow'd of the sun:
Yet shall he mount, and keep his distant way
Beyond the limits of a vulgar fate,
Beneath the Good how far--but far above the Great.

**THE BARD**
A Pindaric Ode.

I. I
"Ruin seize thee, ruthless King!
Confusion on thy banners wait;
Tho' fann'd by Conquest's crimson wing,
They mock the air with idle state.
Helm, nor hauberk's twisted mail,
Nor e'en thy virtues, Tyrant, shall avail
To save thy secret soul from nightly fears,
From Cambria's curse, from Cambria's tears!"
Such were the sounds that o'er the crested pride
Of the first Edward scatter'd wild dismay,
As down the steep of Snowdon's shaggy side
He wound with toilsome march his long array.
Stout Gloster stood aghast in speechless trance:
"To arms!" cried Mortimer, and couch'd his quivering lance.

I. II
On a rock whose haughty brow
Frowns o'er old Conway's foaming flood,
Rob'd in the sable garb of woe,
With haggard eyes the poet stood
(Loose his beard, and hoary hair
Stream'd, like a meteor, to the troubled air),
And with a master's hand, and prophet's fire,
Struck the deep sorrows of his lyre.
"Hark, how each giant oak, and desert cave,
Sighs to the torrent's awful voice beneath!
O'er thee, O King! their hundred arms they wave,
Revenge on thee in hoarser murmurs breathe;
Vocal no more, since Cambria's fatal day,
To high-born Hoel's harp, or soft Llewellyn's lay.

I. III
"Cold is Cadwallo's tongue,
That hush'd the stormy main;
Brave Urien sleeps upon his craggy bed;
Mountains, ye mourn in vain
Modred, whose magic song
Made huge Plinlimmon bow his cloud-topt head.
On dreary Arvon's shore they lie,
Smear'd with gore, and ghastly pale:
Far, far aloof th' affrighted ravens sail;
The famish'd eagle screams, and passes by.
Dear lost companions of my tuneful art,
Dear as the light that visits these sad eyes,
Dear as the ruddy drops that warm my heart,

Ye died amidst your dying country's cries
No more I weep. They do not sleep.
On yonder cliffs, a grisly band,
I see them sit, they linger yet,
Avengers of their native land:
With me in dreadful harmony they join,
And weave with bloody hands the tissue of thy line.

II. I
"Weave the warp, and weave the woof,
The winding-sheet of Edward's race.
Give ample room, and verge enough
The characters of hell to trace.
Mark the year, and mark the night,
When Severn shall reëcho with affright
The shrieks of death thro' Berkeley's roofs that ring,
Shrieks of an agonizing king!
She-wolf of France, with unrelenting fangs,
That tear'st the bowels of thy mangled mate,
From thee be born, who o'er thy country hangs
The scourge of heaven. What terrors round him wait!
Amazement in his van, with Flight combin'd,
And Sorrow's faded form, and Solitude behind.

II. II
"Mighty victor, mighty lord!
Low on his funeral couch he lies!
No pitying heart, no eye, afford
A tear to grace his obsequies.
Is the sable warrior fled?
Thy son is gone. He rests among the dead.
The swarm that in thy noontide beam were born?
Gone to salute the rising morn.
Fair laughs the morn, and soft the zephyr blows,
While proudly riding o'er the azure realm
In gallant trim the gilded vessel goes;
Youth on the prow, and Pleasure at the helm;
Regardless of the sweeping whirlwind's sway,
That, hush'd in grim repose, expects his evening prey.

II. III
"Fill high the sparkling bowl,
The rich repast prepare;
Reft of a crown, he yet may share the feast:
Close by the regal chair
Fell Thirst and Famine scowl
A baleful smile upon their baffled guest.
Heard ye the din of battle bray,
Lance to lance, and horse to horse?
Long years of havoc urge their destined course,
And thro' the kindred squadrons mow their way.

Ye towers of Julius, London's lasting shame,
With many a foul and midnight murther fed,
Revere his consort's faith, his father's fame,
And spare the meek usurper's holy head.
Above, below, the rose of snow,
Twin'd with her blushing foe, we spread:
The bristled boar in infant gore
Wallows beneath the thorny shade.
Now, brothers, bending o'er the accursed loom,
Stamp we our vengeance deep, and ratify his doom.

III. I
"Edward, lo! to sudden fate
(Weave we the woof. The thread is spun.)
Half of thy heart we consecrate.
(The web is wove. The work is done.)
Stay, oh stay! nor thus forlorn
Leave me unbless'd, unpitied, here to mourn:
In yon bright track, that fires the western skies,
They melt, they vanish from my eyes.
But oh! what solemn scenes on Snowdon's height
Descending slow their glittering skirts unroll?
Visions of glory, spare my aching sight!
Ye unborn ages, crowd not on my soul!
No more our long-lost Arthur we bewail.
All hail, ye genuine kings, Britannia's issue, hail!

III. II
"Girt with many a baron bold
Sublime their starry fronts they rear;
And gorgeous dames, and statesmen old
In bearded majesty, appear.
In the midst a form divine!
Her eye proclaims her of the Briton line;
Her lion-port, her awe-commanding face,
Attemper'd sweet to virgin-grace.
What strings symphonious tremble in the air,
What strains of vocal transport round her play!
Hear from the grave, great Taliessin, hear;
They breathe a soul to animate thy clay.
Bright Rapture calls, and soaring as she sings,
Waves in the eye of heaven her many-colour'd wings.

III. III
"The verse adorn again
Fierce War, and faithful Love,
And Truth severe, by fairy Fiction drest.
In buskin'd measures move
Pale Grief, and pleasing Pain,
With Horror, tyrant of the throbbing breast.
A voice, as of the cherub-choir,

Gales from blooming Eden bear;
And distant warblings lessen on my ear,
That lost in long futurity expire.
Fond impious man, think'st thou yon sanguine cloud,
Rais'd by thy breath, has quench'd the orb of day?
To-morrow he repairs the golden flood,
And warms the nations with redoubled ray.
Enough for me; with joy I see
The different doom our fates assign.
Be thine despair, and sceptred care;
To triumph, and to die, are mine."
He spoke, and headlong from the mountain's height
Deep in the roaring tide he plung'd to endless night.


HYMN TO ADVERSITY.

Daughter of Jove, relentless power,
Thou tamer of the human breast,
Whose iron scourge and torturing hour
The bad affright, afflict the best!
Bound in thy adamantine chain,
The proud are taught to taste of pain,
And purple tyrants vainly groan
With pangs unfelt before, unpitied and alone.

When first thy sire to send on earth
Virtue, his darling child, design'd,
To thee he gave the heavenly birth,
And bade to form her infant mind.
Stern rugged nurse! thy rigid lore
With patience many a year she bore:
What sorrow was, thou bad'st her know,
And from her own she learn'd to melt at others' woe.

Scar'd at thy frown terrific, fly
Self-pleasing Folly's idle brood,
Wild Laughter, Noise, and thoughtless Joy,
And leave us leisure to be good.
Light they disperse, and with them go
The summer friend, the flattering foe;
By vain Prosperity receiv'd,
To her they vow their truth, and are again believ'd.

Wisdom in sable garb array'd,
Immersed in rapturous thought profound,
And Melancholy, silent maid,
With leaden eye that loves the ground,
Still on thy solemn steps attend;
Warm Charity, the general friend,
With Justice, to herself severe,

And Pity, dropping soft the sadly-pleasing tear.

Oh! gently on thy suppliant's head,
Dread goddess, lay thy chastening hand!
Not in thy Gorgon terrors clad,
Not circled with the vengeful band
(As by the impious thou art seen),
With thundering voice and threatening mien,
With screaming Horror's funeral cry,
Despair, and fell Disease, and ghastly Poverty:

Thy form benign, O goddess, wear,
Thy milder influence impart;
Thy philosophic train be there
To soften, not to wound, my heart.
The generous spark extinct revive,
Teach me to love and to forgive,
Exact my own defects to scan,
What others are to feel, and know myself a Man.

"Mark the year, and mark the night,
When Severn shall reëcho with affright
The shrieks of death thro' Berkeley's roofs that ring,
Shrieks of an agonizing king!"


TOPHET
Inscription on a portrait.

Such Tophet was; so looked the grinning fiend
Whom many a frighted prelate called his friend;
I saw them bow and, while they wished him dead,
With servile simper nod the mitred head.
Our Mother-Church with half-averted sight
Blushed as she blessed her grisly proselyte:
Hosannahs rung through Hell's tremendous borders,
And Satan's self had thoughts of taking orders.


SKETCH OF HIS OWN CHARACTER
Too poor for a bribe and too proud to importune,
He had not the method of making a fortune:
Could love and could hate, so was thought somewhat odd;
No very great wit, he believed in a God.
A post or a pension he did not desire,
But left church and state to Charles Townshend and Squire.

LINES WRITTEN AT BURNHAM
And, as they bow their hoary tops, relate
In murmuring sounds the dark decrees of fate;
While visions, as poetic eyes avow,
Cling to each leaf and swarm on every bough:


LINES SPOKEN BY THE GHOST OF JOHN DENNIS AT THE DEVIL TAVERN
From purling streams and the Elysian scene,
From groves that smile with never-fading green,
I reascend: in Atropos' despite
Restored to Celadon and upper light.
Ye gods, that sway the regions under ground,
Reveal to mortal view your realms profound;
At his command admit the eye of day:
When Celadon commands, what god can disobey?
Nor seeks he your Tartarean fires to know,
The house of torture and the abyss of woe;
But happy fields and mansions free from pain,
Gay meads and springing flowers, best please the gentle swain.

That little, naked, melancholy thing,
My soul, when first she tried her flight to wing,
Began with speed new regions to explore,
And blundered through a narrow postern door.
First most devoutly having said its prayers,
It tumbled down a thousand pair of stairs,
Through entries long, through cellars vast and deep,
Where ghostly rats their habitations keep,
Where spiders spread their webs and owlish goblins sleep.
After so many chances had befell,
It came into a mead of asphodel:
Betwixt the confines of the light and dark
It lies, of 'Lysium the St. James's Park.
Here spirit-beaux flutter along the Mall,
And shadows in disguise skate o'er the iced Canal;
Here groves embowered and more sequestered shades,
Frequented by the ghosts of ancient maids,
Are seen to rise. The melancholy scene,
With gloomy haunts and twilight walks between,
Conceals the wayward band: here spend their time
Greensickness girls that died in youthful prime,
Virgins forlorn, all dressed in willow-green-i,
With Queen Elizabeth and Nicolini.

More to reveal, or many words to use,
Would tire alike your patience and my muse.
Believe that never was so faithful found
Queen Proserpine to Pluto under ground,
Or Cleopatra to her Mark Antony,

As Orozmades to his Celadony.

P.S. Lucrece for half a crown will show you fun,
But Mrs. Oldfield is become a nun.
Nobles and cits, Prince Pluto and his spouse,
Flock to the ghost of Covent-Garden House:
Plays, which were hissed above, below revive,
When dead applauded that were damned alive.
The people, as in life, still keep their passions,
But differ something from the world in fashions.
Queen Artemisia breakfasts on bohea,
And Alexander wears a ramilie.


EPITAPH ON SIR WILLIAM WILLIAMS
Here, foremost in the dangerous paths of fame,
Young Williams fought for England's fair renown;
His mind each Muse, each Grace adorned his frame,
Nor Envy dared to view him with a frown.

At Aix uncalled his maiden sword he drew,
(There first in blood his infant glory sealed);
From fortune, pleasure, science, love, he flew,
And scorned repose when Britain took the field.

With eyes of flame and cool intrepid breast,
Victor he stood on Belle Isle's rocky steeps;
Ah gallant youth! this marble tells the rest,
Where melancholy Friendship bends and weeps.


EPITAPH ON MRS MASON
Tell them, though 'tis an awful thing to die
('Twas ev'n to thee) yet the dread path once trod,
Heaven lifts its everlasting portals high
And bids "the pure in heart behold their God."


EPITAPH ON MRS CLERKE
Lo! where this silent marble weeps,
A friend, a wife, a mother sleeps:
A heart, within whose sacred cell
The peaceful virtues loved to dwell.
Affection warm, and faith sincere,
And soft humanity were there.
In agony, in death, resigned,
She felt the wound she left behind.
Her infant image, here below,

Sits smiling on a father's woe:
Whom what awaits, while yet he strays
Along the lonely vale of days?
A pang, to secret sorrow dear;
A sigh; an unavailing tear;
Till time shall every grief remove,
With life, with memory, and with love.


EPITAPH ON A CHILD
Here, freed from pain, secure from misery, lies
A child, the darling of his parents' eyes:
A gentler lamb ne'er sported on the plain,
A fairer flower will never bloom again.
Few were the days allotted to his breath;
Now let him sleep in peace his night of death.


THE CANDIDATE
When sly Jemmy Twitcher had smugged up his face
With a lick of court whitewash and pious grimace,
A-wooing he went, where three sisters of old
In harmless society guttle and scold.

'Lord! Sister,' says Physic to Law, 'I declare
Such a sheep-biting look, such a pick-pocket air,
Not I, for the Indies! you know I'm no prude;
But his nose is a shame and his eyes are so lewd!
Then he shambles and straddles so oddly, I fear
No; at our time of life, 'twould be silly, my dear.'

'I don't know,' says Law, 'now methinks, for his look,
'Tis just like the picture in Rochester's book.
But his character, Phyzzy, his morals, his life;
When she died, I can't tell, but he once had a wife.

'They say he's no Christian, loves drinking and whoring,
And all the town rings of his swearing and roaring,
His lying and filching, and Newgate-bird tricks:
Not I,— for a coronet, chariot and six.'

Divinity heard, between waking and dozing,
Her sisters denying and Jemmy proposing;
From dinner she rose with her bumper in hand,
She stroked up her belly and stroked down her band.

'What a pother is here about wenching and roaring!
Why David loved catches and Solomon whoring.
Did not Israel filch from the Egyptians of old

Their jewels of silver and jewels of gold?
The prophet of Bethel, we read, told a lie;
He drinks: so did Noah; he swears: so do I.
To refuse him for such peccadillos were odd;
Besides, he repents, and he talks about God.

'Never hang down your head, you poor penitent elf!
Come, buss me, I'll be Mrs Twitcher myself.
Damn ye both for a couple of Puritan bitches!
He's Christian enough that repents and that stitches.'


## LINES ON THE ACCESSION OF GEORGE III
The Old One's dead,
And in his stead,
The New One takes his place;
Then sing and sigh,
And laugh and cry,
With dismal cheerful face.


## SATIRE ON THE HEADS OF HOUSES; OR, NEVER A BARREL THE BETTER HERRING
O Cambridge, attend
To the satire I've penned
On the heads of thy Houses,
Thou seat of the Muses!
Know the Master of Jesus
Does hugely displease us;
The Master of Maudlin
In the same dirt is dawdling;
The Master of Sidney
Is of the same kidney;
The Master of Trinity
To him bears affinity;
As the Master of Keys
Is as like as two peas,
So the Master of Queen's
Is as like as two beans;
The Master of King's
Copies them in all things;
The Master of Catherine
Takes them all for his pattern;
The Master of Clare
Hits them all to a hair;
The Master of Christ
By the rest is enticed;
But the Master of Emmanuel
Follows them like a spaniel;
The Master of Benet

Is of the like tenet;
The Master of Pembroke
Has from them his system took;
The Master of Peter's
Has all the same features;
The Master of St John's
Like the rest of the dons.

P.S. —As to Trinity Hall
We say nothing at all.


THE PROGRESS OF POESY
Awake, Aeolian lyre, awake,
And give to rapture all thy trembling strings.
From Helicon's harmonious springs
A thousand rills their mazy progress take:
The laughing flowers that round them blow
Drink life and fragrance as they flow.
Now the rich stream of Music winds along,
Deep, majestic, smooth, and strong,
Thro' verdant vales, and Ceres' golden reign;
Now rolling down the steep amain,
Headlong, impetuous, see it pour;
The rocks and nodding groves re-bellow to the roar.

Oh! Sov'reign of the willing soul,
Parent of sweet and solemn-breathing airs,
Enchanting shell! the sullen Cares
And frantic Passions hear thy soft control.
On Thracia's hills the Lord of War
Has curbed the fury of his car,
And dropt his thirsty lance at thy command.
Perching on the sceptred hand
Of Jove, thy magic lulls the feathered king
With ruffled plumes and flagging wing:
Quenched in dark clouds of slumber lie
The terror of his beak, and lightnings of his eye.

Thee the voice, the dance, obey,
Tempered to thy warbled lay.
O'er Idalia's velvet-green
The rosy-crowned Loves are seen
On Cytherea's day,
With antic Sport, and blue-eyed Pleasures,
Frisking light in frolic measures;
Now pursuing, now retreating,
Now in circling troops they meet:
To brisk notes in cadence beating
Glance their many-twinkling feet.

Slow melting strains their Queen's approach declare:
Where'er she turns the Graces homage pay.
With arms sublime that float upon the air
In gliding state she wins her easy way:
O'er her warm cheek and rising bosom move
The bloom of young Desire and purple light of Love.

Man's feeble race what ills await!
Labour, and Penury, the racks of Pain,
Disease, and Sorrow's weeping train,
And Death, sad refuge from the storms of Fate!
The fond complaint, my song, disprove,
And justify the laws of Jove.
Say, has he giv'n in vain the heav'nly Muse?
Night and all her sickly dews,
Her sceptres wan, and birds of boding cry,
He gives to range the dreary sky;
Till down the eastern cliffs afar
Hyperion's march they spy, and glitt'ring shafts of war.

In climes beyond the solar road,
Where shaggy forms o'er ice-built mountains roam,
The Muse has broke the twilight gloom
To cheer the shivering Native's dull abode.
And oft, beneath the od'rous shade
Of Chili's boundless forests laid,
She deigns to hear the savage youth repeat,
In loose numbers wildly sweet,
Their feather-cinctured chiefs, and dusky loves.
Her track, where'er the Goddess roves,
Glory pursue, and gen'rous Shame,
Th' unconquerable Mind, and Freedom's holy flame.

Woods, that wave o'er Delphi's steep,
Isles, that crown th' Aegean deep,
Fields that cool Ilissus laves,
Or where Maeander's amber waves
In lingering lab'rinths creep,
How do your tuneful echoes languish,
Mute, but to the voice of anguish!
Where each old poetic mountain
Inspiration breathed around;
Ev'ry shade and hallowed fountain
Murmured deep a solemn sound:
Till the sad Nine, in Greece's evil hour,
Left their Parnassus for the Latian plains.
Alike they scorn the pomp of tyrant Power,
And coward Vice, that revels in her chains.
When Latium had her lofty spirit lost,
They sought, Oh Albion! next thy sea-encircled coast.

Far from the sun and summer-gale,
In thy green lap was Nature's Darling laid,
What time, where lucid Avon strayed,
To him the mighty mother did unveil
Her awful face: the dauntless child
Stretched forth his little arms, and smiled.
"This pencil take (she said), whose colours clear
Richly paint the vernal year:
Thine too these golden keys, immortal Boy!
This can unlock the gates of Joy;
Of Horror that, and thrilling Fears,
Or ope the sacred source of sympathetic Tears."

Nor second he, that rode sublime
Upon the seraph-wings of Ecstasy,
The secrets of th' Abyss to spy.
He passed the flaming bounds of place and time:
The living Throne, the sapphire-blaze,
Where Angels tremble while they gaze,
He saw; but, blasted with excess of light,
Closed his eyes in endless night.
Behold where Dryden's less presumptuous car
Wide o'er the fields of glory bear
Two coursers of ethereal race,
With necks in thunder clothed, and long-resounding pace.

Hark, his hands the lyre explore!
Bright-eyed Fancy, hovering o'er,
Scatters from her pictured urn
Thoughts that breathe, and words that burn.
But ah! 'tis heard no more -
Oh! Lyre divine, what daring Spirit
Wakes thee now? Though he inherit
Nor the pride, nor ample pinion,
That the Theban eagle bear,
Sailing with supreme dominion
Through the azure deep of air:
Yet oft before his infant eyes would run
Such forms as glitter in the Muse's ray,
With orient hues, unborrowed of the Sun:
Yet shall he mount, and keep his distant way
Beyond the limits of a vulgar fate,
Beneath the Good how far -but far above the Great


### THE FATAL SISTERS

Now the storm begins to lower,
(Haste, the loom of Hell prepares!)
Iron-sleet of arrowy shower
Hurtles in the darkened air.

Glittering lances are the loom,
Where the dusky warp we strain,
Weaving many a soldier's doom,
Orkney's woe and Randver's bane.

See the grisly texture grow,
('Tis of human entrails made!)
And the weights that play below,
Each a gasping warrior's head.

Shafts for shuttles, dipped in gore,
Shoot the trembling cords along.
Sword, that once a monarch bore,
Keep the tissue close and strong.

Mista, black, terrific maid,
Sangrida, and Hilda, see,
Join the wayward work to aid;
'Tis the woof of victory.

Ere the ruddy sun be set,
Pikes must shiver, javelins sing,
Blade with clattering buckler meet,
Hauberk crash, and helmet ring.

(Weave the crimson web of war!)
Let us go, and let us fly
Where our friends the conflict share,
Where they triumph, where they die.

As the paths of fate we tread,
Wading through the ensanguined field,
Gondula and Geira, spread
O'er the youthful king your shield.

We the reins to slaughter give;
Ours to kill, and ours to spare;
Spite the dangers he shall live.
(Weave the crimson web of war!)

They whom once the desert beach
Pent within its bleak domain,
Soon their ample sway shall stretch
O'er the plenty of the plain.

Low the dauntless earl is laid,
Gored with many a gaping wound;
Fate demands a nobler head;
Soon a king shall bite the ground.

Long his loss shall Eirin weep
Ne'er again his likeness see;
Long her strains in sorrow steep,
Strains of immortality!

Horror covers all the heath;
Clouds of carnage blot the sun.
Sisters, weave the web of death;
Sisters, cease, the work is done.

Hail the task, and hail the hands!
Songs of joy and triumph sing!
Joy to the victorious bands
Triumph to the younger king.

Mortal, thou that hear'st the tale,
Learn the tenor of our song.
Scotland, through each winding vale
Far and wide the notes prolong.

Sisters, hence with spurs of speed;
Each her thundering falchion wield;
Each bestride her sable steed.
Hurry, hurry to the field!


THE CURSE UPON EDWARD
Weave the warp, and weave the woof,
The winding-sheet of Edward's race.
Give ample room, and verge enough
The characters of hell to trace.
Mark the year, and mark the night,
When Severn shall re-echo with affright
The shrieks of death, thro' Berkley's roofs that ring,
Shrieks of an agonizing King!
She-wolf of France, with unrelenting fangs,
That tear'st the bowels of thy mangled mate,
From thee be born, who o'er thy country hangs
The scourge of Heav'n. What terrors round him wait!
Amazement in his van, with Flight combined,
And Sorrow's faded form, and Solitude behind.

Mighty Victor, mighty Lord!
Low on his funeral couch he lies!
No pitying heart, no eye, afford
A tear to grace his obsequies.
Is the sable warrior fled?
Thy son is gone. He rests among the dead.
The swarm that in thy noon tide beam were born?
Gone to salute the rising morn.

Fair laughs the morn, and soft the zephyr blows,
While proudly riding o'er the azure realm
In gallant trim the gilded vessel goes;
Youth on the prow, and Pleasure at the helm;
Regardless of the sweeping whirlwind's sway,
That, hush'd in grim repose, expects his evening prey.

Fill high the sparkling bowl,
The rich repast prepare;
Reft of a crown, he yet may share the feast:
Close by the regal chair
Fell Thirst and Famine scowl
A baleful smile upon their baffled guest.
Heard ye the din of battle bray,
Lance to lance, and horse to horse?
Long years of havoc urge their destined course,
And thro' the kindred squadrons mow their way.
Ye Towers of Julius, London's lasting shame,
With many a foul and midnight murder fed,
Revere his consort's faith, his father's fame,
And spare the meek usurper's holy head.
Above, below, the rose of snow,
Twined with her blushing foe, we spread:
The bristled boar in infant-gore
Wallows beneath the thorny shade.
Now, brothers, bending o'er th' accursed loom
Stamp we our vengeance deep, and ratify his doom.

Edward, lo! to sudden fate
(Weave we the woof. The thread is spun)
Half of thy heart we consecrate.
(The web is wove. The work is done.)


SONNET ON THE DEATH OF MR RICHARD WEST
In vain to me the smiling mornings shine,
And redd'ning Phoebus lifts his golden fire:
The birds in vain their amorous descant join;
Or cheerful fields resume their green attire:
These ears, alas! for other notes repine,
A different object do these eyes require:
My lonely anguish melts no heart but mine;
And in my breast the imperfect joys expire.
Yet morning smiles the busy race to cheer,
And new-born pleasure brings to happier men:
The fields to all their wonted tribute bear;
To warm their little loves the birds complain:
I fruitless mourn to him that cannot hear,
And weep the more, because I weep in vain.

## ODE ON THE PLEASURE ARISING FROM VICISSITUDE

Now the golden Morn aloft
Waves her dew-bespangled wing,
With vermeil cheek, and whisper soft
She woos the tardy Spring:
Till April starts, and calls around
The sleeping fragrance from the ground;
And lightly o'er the living scene
Scatters his freshest, tenderest green.

New-born flocks, in rustic dance,
Frisking ply their feeble feet;
Forgetful of their wintry trance
The birds his presence greet:
But chief, the skylark warbles high
His trembling thrilling ecstasy;
And, lessening from the dazzled sight,
Melts into air and liquid light.

Rise, my soul! on wings of fire,
Rise the rapt'rous choir among;
Hark! 'tis Nature strikes the lyre,
And leads the general song:

... Yesterday the sullen year
Saw the snowy whirlwind fly;
Mute was the music of the air,
The herd stood drooping by:
Their raptures now that wildly flow,
No yesterday, nor morrow know;
'Tis man alone that joy descries
With forward, and reverted eyes.

Smiles on past Misfortune's brow
Soft Reflection's hand can trace;
And o'er the cheek of Sorrow throw
A melancholy grace;
While Hope prolongs our happier hour
Or deepest shades, that dimly lower
And blacken round our weary way,
Gilds with a gleam of distant day.

Still, where rosy Pleasure leads,
See a kindred Grief pursue;
Behind the steps that Misery treads,
Approaching Comfort view:
The hues of bliss more brightly glow,
Chastis'd by sabler tints of woe;
And blended form, with artful strife,

The strength and harmony of life.

See the wretch, that long has tost
On the thorny bed of pain,
At length repair his vigour lost,
And breathe, and walk again:
The meanest flow'ret of the vale,
The simplest note that swells the gale,
The common sun, the air, the skies,
To him are opening Paradise.

Humble Quiet builds her cell,
Near the source whence Pleasure flows;
She eyes the clear crystalline well,
And tastes it as it goes.


ODE ON A DISTANT PROSPECT OF ETON COLLEGE
Ye distant spires, ye antique towers,
That crown the watry glade,
Where grateful Science still adores
Her Henry's holy shade;
And ye that from the stately brow
Of Windsor's height th' expanse below
Of grove, of lawn, of mead survey,
Whose turf, whose shade, whose flowers among
Wanders the hoary Thames along
His silver-winding way.

Ah, happy hills, ah, pleasing shade,
Ah fields beloved in vain,
Where once my careless childhood strayed,
A stranger yet to pain!
I feel the gales, that from ye blow,
A momentary bliss bestow,
As waving fresh their gladsome wing,
My weary soul they seem to soothe,
And, redolent of youth,
To breathe a second spring.

Say, Father Thames, for thou hast seen
Full many a sprightly race
Disporting on thy margent green
The paths of pleasure trace,
Who foremost now delight to cleave
With pliant arm thy glassy wave?
The captive linnet which enthrall?
What idle progeny succeed
To chase the rolling circle's speed,
Or urge the flying ball?

While some on earnest business bent
Their murm'ring laborsÊ play
'Gainst graver hours, that bring constraint
To sweeten liberty:
Some bold adventurers disdain
The limits of their little reign,
And unknown regions dare descry:
Still as they run they look behind,
And hear a voice in every wind,
And snatch a fearful joy.

Gay hope is theirs by fancy fed,
Less pleasing when possessed;
The tear forgot as soon as shed,
The sunshine of the breast:
Theirs buxom health of rosy hue,
Wild wit, invention ever-new,
And lively cheer of vigor born;
The thoughtless day, the easy night,
The spirits pure, the slumbers light,
That fly th' approach of morn.

Alas, regardless of their doom,
The little victims play!
No sense have they of ills to come,
Nor care beyond today:
Yet see how all around 'em wait
The ministers of human fate,
And black Misfortune's baleful train!
Ah, show them, where in ambush stand
To seize their prey the murth'rous band!
Ah, tell them, they are men!

These shall the fury Passions tear,
The vultures of the mind,
Disdainful Anger, pallid Fear,
And Shame that skulks behind;
Or pining Love shall waste their youth,
Or Jealousy with rankling tooth,
That inly gnaws the secret heart,
And Envy wan, and faded Care,
Grim-visaged comfortless Despair,
And Sorrow's piercing dart.

Ambition this shall tempt to rise,
Then whirl the wretch from high,
To bitter Scorn a sacrifice,
And grinning Infamy.
The stings of Falsehood those shall try,
And hard Unkindness's altered eye,

That mocks the tear it forced to flow;
And keen Remorse with blood defiled,
And moody Madness laughing wild
Amid severest woe.

Lo, in the vale of years beneath
A grisly troop are seen,
The painful family of Death,
More hideous than their Queen:
This racks the joints, this fires the veins,
That every laboring sinew strains,
Those in the deeper vitals rage:
Lo, Poverty, to fill the band,
That numbs the soul with icy hand,
And slow-consuming Age.

To each his suff'rings: all are men,
Condemned alike to groan;
The tender for another's pain,
Th' unfeeling for his own.
Yet ah! why should they know their fate?
Since sorrow never comes too late,
And happiness too swiftly flies.
Thought would destroy their paradise.
No more; where ignorance is bliss,
'Tis folly to be wise.

## THE LIFE OF THOMAS GRAY

### BY ROBERT CARRUTHERS.

Thomas Gray, the author of the celebrated Elegy written in a Country Churchyard, was born in Cornhill, London, December 26, 1716. His father, Philip Gray, an exchange broker and scrivener, was a wealthy and nominally respectable citizen, but he treated his family with brutal severity and neglect, and the poet was altogether indebted for the advantages of a learned education to the affectionate care and industry of his mother, whose maiden name was Antrobus, and who, in conjunction with a maiden sister, kept a millinery shop. A brother of Mrs. Gray was assistant to the Master of Eton, and was also a fellow of Pembroke College, Cambridge. Under his protection the poet was educated at Eton, and from thence went to Peterhouse, attending college from 1734 to September, 1738. At Eton he had as contemporaries Richard West, son of the Lord Chancellor of Ireland, and Horace Walpole, son of the triumphant Whig minister, Sir Robert Walpole. West died early in his 26th year, but his genius and virtues and his sorrows will forever live in the correspondence of his friend. In the spring of 1739, Gray was invited by Horace Walpole to accompany him as travelling companion in a tour through France and Italy. They made the usual route, and Gray wrote remarks on all he saw in Florence, Rome, Naples, etc. His observations on arts and antiquities, and his sketches of foreign manners, evince his admirable taste, learning, and discrimination. Since Milton, no such accomplished English traveller had visited those classic shores. In their journey through Dauphiny, Gray's attention was strongly arrested by the wild and picturesque site of the Grande Chartreuse, surrounded by its dense forest of beech and fir, its enormous precipices, cliffs, and cascades. He visited it a second time on his return, and in the album of the mountain convent he wrote his famous Alcaic Ode. At Reggio the travellers quarrelled and parted. Walpole took the whole blame on himself. He was fond of pleasure and amusements, "intoxicated by vanity, indulgence, and the insolence of his situation as a prime minister's son" his own confession, while Gray was studious, of a serious disposition, and independent spirit. The immediate cause of the rupture is said to have been Walpole's clandestinely opening, reading, and resealing a letter addressed to Gray, in which he expected to find a confirmation of his suspicions that Gray had been writing unfavourably of him to some friends in England. A partial reconciliation was effected about three years afterwards by the intervention of a lady, and Walpole redeemed his youthful error by a life-long sincere admiration and respect for his friend. From Reggio Gray proceeded to Venice, and thence travelled homewards, attended by a laquais de voyage. He arrived in England in September, 1741, having been absent about two years and a half. His father died in November, and it was found that the poet's fortune would not enable him to prosecute the study of the law. He therefore retired to Cambridge, and fixed his residence at the university. There he continued for the remainder of his life, with the exception of about two years spent in London, when the treasures of the British Museum were thrown open. At Cambridge he had the range of noble libraries. His happiness consisted in study, and he perused with critical attention the Greek and Roman poets, philosophers, historians, and orators. Plato and the Anthologia he read and annotated with great care, as if for publication. He compiled tables of Greek chronology, added notes to Linnæus and other naturalists, wrote geographical disquisitions on Strabo; and, besides being familiar with French and Italian literature, was a zealous archæological student, and profoundly versed in architecture, botany, painting, and music. In all departments of human learning, except mathematics, he was a master. But it follows that one so studious, so critical, and so fastidious, could not be a voluminous writer. A few poems include all the original compositions of Gray, the quintessence, as it were, of thirty years of ceaseless study and contemplation, irradiated by bright and fitful gleams of inspiration. In 1742 Gray composed his Ode to Spring, his Ode on a Distant Prospect of Eton College, and his Ode to Adversity, productions which most readers of poetry can repeat from memory. He commenced a didactic poem, On the Alliance of Education and Government, but wrote only about a hundred lines. Every reader must regret that this philosophical poem is but a fragment. It is in the style and measure of Dryden, of whom Gray was an ardent admirer and close student. His Elegy written in a Country Churchyard was completed and published in 1751. In the form of a sixpenny brochure it circulated rapidly, four editions being exhausted the first year. This popularity surprised the poet. He said sarcastically that it was owing entirely to the subject, and that the public would have received it as well if it had been written in prose. The solemn and affecting nature of the poem, applicable to all ranks and classes, no doubt aided its sale; it required high poetic sensibility and a cultivated taste to appreciate the rapid transitions, the figurative language, and lyrical magnificence of the odes; but the elegy went home to all hearts; while its musical harmony, originality, and pathetic train of sentiment and feeling render it one of the most perfect of English poems. No vicissitudes of taste or fashion have affected its popularity. When the original manuscript of the poem was lately (1854) offered for sale, it brought the almost incredible sum of 131 pounds. The two great odes of Gray, The Progress of Poetry and The Bard, were published in 1757, and were but coldly received. His name, however, stood high, and on the death of Cibber, the same year, he was offered the laureateship, which he wisely declined. He was ambitious, however, of obtaining the more congenial and dignified appointment of Professor of Modern History in the University of Cambridge, which fell vacant in 1762, and, by the advice of his friends, he made application to Lord Bute, but was unsuccessful. Lord Bute had designed it for the tutor of his son-in-law, Sir James Lowther. No one had heard of the tutor, but the Bute influence was all-prevailing. In 1765 Gray took a journey into Scotland, penetrating as far north as Dunkeld and the Pass of Killiecrankie; and his account of his tour, in letters to his friends, is replete with interest and with touches of his peculiar humour and graphic description. One other poem proceeded from his pen. In 1768 the Professorship of Modern History was again vacant, and the Duke of Grafton bestowed it upon Gray. A sum of 400 pounds per annum was thus added to his income; but his health was precarious, he had lost it, he said, just when he began to be easy in his circumstances. The nomination of the Duke of Grafton to the office of Chancellor of the University enabled Gray to acknowledge the favour conferred on himself. He thought it better that gratitude should sing than expectation, and he honoured his grace's installation with an ode.

Such occasional productions are seldom happy; but Gray preserved his poetic dignity and select beauty of expression. He made the founders of Cambridge, as Mr. Hallam has remarked, "pass before our eyes like shadows over a magic glass." When the ceremony of the installation was over, the poet-professor went on a tour to the lakes of Cumberland and Westmoreland, and few of the beauties of the lake-country, since so famous, escaped his observation. This was to be his last excursion. While at dinner one day in the college-hall he was seized with an attack of gout in his stomach, which resisted all the powers of medicine, and proved fatal in less than a week. He died on the 30th of July, 1771, and was buried, according to his own desire, beside the remains of his mother at Stoke-Pogis, near Slough, in Buckinghamshire, in a beautiful sequestered village churchyard that is supposed to have furnished the scene of his elegy.[1] The literary habits and personal peculiarities of Gray are familiar to us from the numerous representations and allusions of his friends. It is easy to fancy the recluse-poet sitting in his college-chambers in the old quadrangle of Pembroke Hall. His windows are ornamented with mignonette and choice flowers in China vases, but outside may be discerned some iron-work intended to be serviceable as a fire-escape, for he has a horror of fire. His furniture is neat and select; his books, rather for use than show, are disposed around him. He has a harpsichord in the room. In the corner of one of the apartments is a trunk containing his deceased mother's dresses, carefully folded up and preserved. His fastidiousness, bordering upon effeminacy, is visible in his gait and manner, in his handsome features and small, well-dressed person, especially when he walks abroad and sinks the author and hard student in "the gentleman who sometimes writes for his amusement." He writes always with a crow-quill, speaks slowly and sententiously, and shuns the crew of dissonant college revellers, who call him "a prig," and seek to annoy him. Long mornings of study, and nights feverish from ill-health, are spent in those chambers; he is often listless and in low spirits; yet his natural temper is not desponding, and he delights in employment. He has always something to learn or to communicate, some sally of humour or quiet stroke of satire for his friends and correspondents, some note on natural history to enter in his journal, some passage of Plato to unfold and illustrate, some golden thought of classic inspiration to inlay on his page, some bold image to tone down, some verse to retouch and harmonize. His life is on the whole innocent and happy, and a feeling of thankfulness to the Great Giver is breathed over all.

[Footnote 1: A claim has been put up for the churchyard of Granchester, about two miles from Cambridge, the great bell of St. Mary's serving for the "curfew." But Stoke-Pogis is more likely to have been the spot, if any individual locality were indicated. The poet often visited the village, his aunt and mother residing there, and his aunt was interred in the churchyard of the place. Gray's epitaph on his mother is characterized not only by the tenderness with which he always regarded her memory, but by his style and cast of thought. It runs thus: "Beside her friend and sister here sleep the remains of Dorothy Gray, widow, the careful, tender mother of many children, one of whom alone had the misfortune to survive her. She died March 11, 1753, aged 72." She had lived to read the Elegy, which was perhaps an ample recompense for her maternal cares and affection. Mrs. Gray's will commences in a similar touching strain: "In the name of God, amen. This is the last will and desire of Dorothy Gray to her son Thomas Gray." [Cunningham's edit. of Johnson's Lives.] They were all in all to each other. The father's cruelty and neglect, their straitened circumstances, the sacrifices made by the mother to maintain her son at the university, her pride in the talents and conduct of that son, and the increasing gratitude and affection of the latter, nursed in his scholastic and cloistered solitude, these form an affecting but noble record in the history of genius.

[One would infer from the above that Mrs. Gray was not "interred in the churchyard of the place," though the epitaph given immediately after shows that she was. Gray in his will directed that he should be laid beside her there. The passage in the will reads thus: "First, I do desire that my body may be deposited in the vault, made by my dear mother in the churchyard of Stoke-Pogeis, near Slough in Buckinghamshire, by her remains, in a coffin of seasoned oak, neither lined nor covered, and (unless it be inconvenient) I could wish that one of my executors may see me laid in the grave, and distribute among such honest and industrious poor persons in said parish as he thinks fit, the sum of ten pounds in charity." Ed.]]

In 1778 a monument to Gray was erected in Westminster Abbey by Mason, with the following inscription:

No more the Grecian muse unrivall'd reigns,
To Britain let the nations homage pay;
She felt a Homer's fire in Milton's strains,
A Pindar's rapture in the lyre of Gray.

The cenotaph afterwards erected in Stoke Park by Mr. Penn is described below.


STOKE-POGIS.

FROM HOWITT'S "HOMES AND HAUNTS OF THE BRITISH POETS."[1]

*[Footnote 1: Harper's edition, vol. i. p. 314 foll.]*

It is at Stoke-Pogis that we seek the most attractive vestiges of Gray. Here he used to spend his vacations, not only when a youth at Eton, but during the whole of his future life, while his mother and his aunts lived. Here it was that his Ode on a Distant Prospect of Eton College, his celebrated Elegy written in a Country Churchyard, and his Long Story were not only written, but were mingled with the circumstances and all the tenderest feelings of his own life.

His mother and aunts lived at an old-fashioned house in a very retired spot at Stoke, called West-End. This house stood in a hollow, much screened by trees. A small stream ran through the garden, and it is said that Gray used to employ himself when here much in this garden, and that many of the trees still remaining are of his planting. On one side of the house extended an upland field, which was planted round so as to give a charming retired walk; and at the summit of the field was raised an artificial mound, and upon it was built a sort of arcade or summer-house, which gave full prospect of Windsor and Eton. Here Gray used to delight to sit; here he was accustomed to read and write much; and it is just the place to inspire the Ode on Eton College, which lay in the midst of its fine landscape, beautifully in view. The old house inhabited by Gray and his mother has just been pulled down, and replaced by an Elizabethan mansion by the present proprietor, Mr. Penn, of Stoke Park, just by.[2] The garden, of course, has shared in the change, and now stands gay with its fountain and its modern greenhouse, and, excepting for some fine trees, no longer reminds you of Gray. The woodland walk still remains round the adjoining field, and the summer-house on its summit, though now much cracked by time, and only held together by iron cramps. The trees are now so lofty that they completely obstruct the view, and shut out both Eton and Windsor.

*[Footnote 2: This was written (or published, at least) in 1846; but Mitford, in the Life of Gray prefixed to the "Eton edition" of his Poems, published in 1847, says: "The house, which is now called West-*

*End, lies in a secluded part of the parish, on the road to Fulmer. It has lately been much enlarged and adorned by its present proprietor [Mr. Penn], but the room called 'Gray's' (distinguished by a small balcony) is still preserved; and a shady walk round an adjoining meadow, with a summer-house on the rising land, are still remembered as favourite places frequented by the poet."*

Stoke Park is about a couple of miles from Slough. The country is flat, but its monotony is broken up by the noble character and disposition of its woods. Near the house is a fine expanse of water, across which the eye falls on fine views, particularly to the south, of Windsor Castle, Cooper's Hill, and the Forest Woods. About three hundred yards from the north front of the house stands a column, sixty-eight feet high, bearing on the top a colossal statue of Sir Edward Coke, by Rosa. The woods of the park shut out the view of West-End House, Gray's occasional residence, but the space is open from the mansion across the park, so as to take in the view both of the church and of a monument erected by the late Mr. Penn to Gray. Alighting from the carriage at a lodge, we enter the park just at the monument. This is composed of fine freestone, and consists of a large sarcophagus, supported on a square pedestal, with inscriptions on each side. Three of them are selected from the Ode on Eton College and the Elegy. They are:

Hard by yon wood, now smiling as in scorn,
Muttering his wayward fancies he would rove;
Now drooping, woeful-wan, like one forlorn,
Or craz'd with care, or cross'd in hopeless love.

One morn I miss'd him on the custom'd hill,
Along the heath, and near his fav'rite tree;
Another came; nor yet beside the rill,
Nor up the lawn, nor at the wood was he.

The second is from the Ode:

Ye distant spires! ye antique towers!
That crown the watery glade,
Where grateful Science still adores
Her Henry's holy shade;
And ye, that from the stately brow
Of Windsor's heights th' expanse below
Of grove, of lawn, of mead survey,
Whose turf, whose shade, whose flowers among
Wanders the hoary Thames along
His silver-winding way.

Ah, happy hills! ah, pleasing shade!
Ah, fields belov'd in vain!
Where once my careless childhood stray'd,
A stranger yet to pain!
I feel the gales that from ye blow,
A momentary bliss bestow.

The third is again from the Elegy:

Beneath those rugged elms, that yew-tree's shade,
Where heaves the turf in many a mouldering heap,

Each in his narrow cell forever laid,
The rude forefathers of the hamlet sleep.

The breezy call of incense-breathing morn,
The swallow twittering from the straw-built shed,
The cock's shrill clarion or the echoing horn,
No more shall rouse them from their lowly bed.

The fourth bears this inscription:

This Monument, in honour of
THOMAS GRAY,
Was erected A.D. 1799,
Among the scenery
Celebrated by that great Lyric and Elegiac Poet.
He died in 1771,
And lies unnoted in the adjoining Church-yard,
Under the Tomb-stone on which he piously
And pathetically recorded the interment
Of his Aunt and lamented Mother.

This monument is in a neatly kept garden-like enclosure, with a winding walk approaching from the shade of the neighbouring trees. To the right, across the park, at some little distance, backed by fine trees, stands the rural little church and churchyard where Gray wrote his Elegy, and where he lies. As you walk on to this, the mansion closes the distant view between the woods with fine effect. The church has often been engraved, and is therefore tolerably familiar to the general reader. It consists of two barn-like structures, with tall roofs, set side by side, and the tower and finely tapered spire rising above them at the northwest corner. The church is thickly hung with ivy, where

"The moping owl may to the moon complain
Of such as, wandering near her secret bower,
Molest her ancient, solitary reign."

The structure is as simple and old-fashioned, both without and within, as any village church can well be. No village, however, is to be seen. Stoke consists chiefly of scattered houses, and this is now in the midst of the park. In the churchyard,

"Beneath those rugged elms, that yew-tree's shade,
Where heaves the turf in many a mouldering heap,
Each in his narrow cell forever laid,
The rude forefathers of the hamlet sleep."

All this is quite literal; and the tomb of the poet himself, near the southeast window, completes the impression of the scene. It is a plain brick altar tomb, covered with a blue slate slab, and, besides his own ashes, contains those of his mother and aunt. On the slab are inscribed the following lines by Gray himself: "In the vault beneath are deposited, in hope of a joyful resurrection, the remains of Mary Antrobus. She died unmarried, Nov. 5, 1749, aged sixty-six. In the same pious confidence, beside her friend and sister, here sleep the remains of Dorothy Gray, widow; the careful, tender mother of many children, ONE of whom alone had the misfortune to survive her. She died, March 11, 1753, aged LXXII."

No testimony of the interment of Gray in the same tomb was inscribed anywhere till Mr. Penn, in 1799, erected the monument already mentioned, and placed a small slab in the wall, under the window, opposite to the tomb itself, recording the fact of Gray's burial there. The whole scene is well worthy of a summer day's stroll, especially for such as, pent in the metropolis, know how to enjoy the quiet freshness of the country and the associations of poetry and the past.

www.ingramcontent.com/pod-product-compliance
Lightning Source LLC
Chambersburg PA
CBHW061518040426
42450CB00008B/1681